A KEEPSAKE JOURNAL

GRANDPA,

Do You Remember When?

Sharing a Lifetime of Loving Memories

HARVEST HOUSE PUBLISHERS
EUGENE, OREGON

PAINTINGS BY
Jim Daly

GRANDPA, *Do You Remember When?*
Copyright © 2007 Harvest House Publishers
Published by Harvest House Publishers
Eugene, Oregon 97402
www.harvesthousepublishers.com

ISBN 978-0-7369-1051-4

Artwork Copyright © by Jim Daly and may not be reproduced without permission. For more information about art prints featured in this book, please contact:

> Jim Daly
> P.O. Box 25146
> Eugene, OR 97402
> www.jimdalyart.com

Design and production by Koechel Peterson & Associates, Inc., Minneapolis, Minnesota

Printed in Singapore

12 13 14 15 16 17/ IM / 13 12 11 10 9 8 7

Grandpa, Do You Remember When?

Grandpa, do you remember when…
You were a boy full of questions and zest?
You sought out adventure,
And pursued every quest.

Running, playing, throwing the ball,
You enjoyed time with friends
Most of all.

Grandpa, do you remember when…
You asked Grandma to be your wife?
You worked hard together
To build a shared life.

Traditions, legacies, and memories formed,
And soon life was enriched
When a child was born.

Grandpa, do you remember when…
You heard the news about me?
Were you surprised that time
Had gone by so quickly!

Laughing, remembering, and sharing will soon start
To make your stories and wisdom
A part of my heart.

Tell me about your life, Grandpa _____

With love,

_____

Grandchildren are God's way of
compensating us for growing old.

Mary H. Waldrip

Our Family Tree

Grandpa, what were the names of your grandma and grandpa?
Your parents? _____

_____

How many brothers and sisters do you have? _____
What are their names and ages? _____

_____

When were your children born? _____

_____

_____

Where does our family come from originally? _____

_____

Share a family story that was told to you as boy. _____

_____

_____

_____

_____

_____

_____

Your Early Days

Grandpa, when is your birthday? _____

_____

_____

Where were you born? _____

_____

_____

How did your mom and dad pick your name? _____

_____

_____

Who was president when you were born? _____

_____

_____

What was your childhood home like? _____

_____

_____

_____

_____

*M*y childhood's home I see again, And sadden with the view;
And still, as memory crowds my brain, There's pleasure in it, too.

Abraham Lincoln, from the poem
"My Childhood's Home I See Again"

*I*t's a pleasure to share one's memories. Everything remembered
is dear, endearing, touching, precious. At least the past is safe—
though we didn't know it at the time. We know it now.
Because it's in the past; because we have survived.

Susan Sontag

Life as a Child

What did you love most about being a child? _____

_____

What is one of your favorite memories about your mom and dad?

_____

_____

Did you have chores to do each day? _____

_____

What were your favorite or your least favorite foods? _____

_____

Did you have a favorite movie or show? _____

_____

How did you like to pass the time during a free afternoon? _____

_____

What was the best place for you to play as a kid? _____

_____

_____

_____

School Days

Grandpa, do you remember when you were a schoolboy? _____

_____

_____

_____

Where was your first school? _____

Who was your best teacher? _____

What were your favorite and least favorite subjects? _____

_____

Did you go to college? What did you study? _____

What kind of activities were you involved
in throughout your school years? _____

_____

_____

_____

_____

_____

You are told a lot about your education, but some beautiful, sacred memory, preserved since childhood, is perhaps the best education of all. If a man carries many such memories into life with him, he is saved for the rest of his days. And even if only one good memory is left in our hearts, it may also be the instrument of our salvation one day.

Fyodor Dostoyevsky

Grandchildren don't stay young forever, which is good because Pop-pops have only so many horsey rides in them.

Gene Perret

Animal Friends

Grandpa, did you take care of animals when you were growing up? _____

_____

What pets did you have as a child? What were their names? _____

_____

If you could've had any kind of pet as a kid, what would you have chosen? _____

_____

_____

Did you let your children have pets? _____

_____

_____

_____

Time for Everything

What is your favorite season of the year, Grandpa? _____

Did you visit your hometown later? How had it changed?
_____

What was that stroll down memory lane like? _____
_____
_____

Which years of your childhood are most dear to you? _____

When did you first think about your future? _____
_____
_____
_____
_____
_____
_____
_____
_____
_____

There is a time for everything, a season for every activity under heaven.

The Book of Ecclesiastes

*I*t is the marriage of the soul with Nature that makes
the intellect fruitful, and gives birth to imagination.

Henry D. Thoreau

Great Outdoors

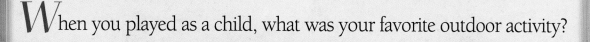

When you played as a child, what was your favorite outdoor activity?

_____

_____

_____

Can you recall the landscape that surrounded you as a child? _____

_____

_____

Did you ever make a fort in the woods? A trail in the meadow?
A tree house? _____

_____

_____

_____

If you could show me one special place in nature, where would it be?

_____

_____

_____

_____

_____

Faith Traditions

*D*id your family go to church when you were a boy? _____

_____

What was your favorite prayer for bedtime and mealtime? _____

_____

_____

What is your favorite verse or memory from church? _____

_____

What is your prayer for me, Grandpa? _____

_____

_____

_____

_____

_____

For the Lord is good. His unfailing love continues forever,
and his faithfulness continues to each generation.

The Book of Psalms

Shared laughter creates a bond of friendships. When people laugh together, they cease to be young and old, teacher and pupils, worker and boss. They become a single group of human beings.

W. Lee Grant

Good Times

*T*ell me about a time when you were really happy.

What hobbies or activities have brought you joy over the years?

Share with me a story from your life that still makes you laugh.

What do you think is the key to happiness?

Take Me Out to the Ball Game

What games did you and your friends play? _____

_____

_____

Did you have a favorite toy? _____

As your children grew up, what games did you play with them?

_____

Do you have a fond memory of attending or participating in a sports event? _____

_____

_____

What game do you hope I learn? _____

_____

_____

_____

_____

You are worried about seeing him spend his early years in doing nothing. What!
Is it nothing to be happy? Nothing to skip, play, and run around all day long?
Never in his life will he be so busy again.

Jean-Jacques Rousseau

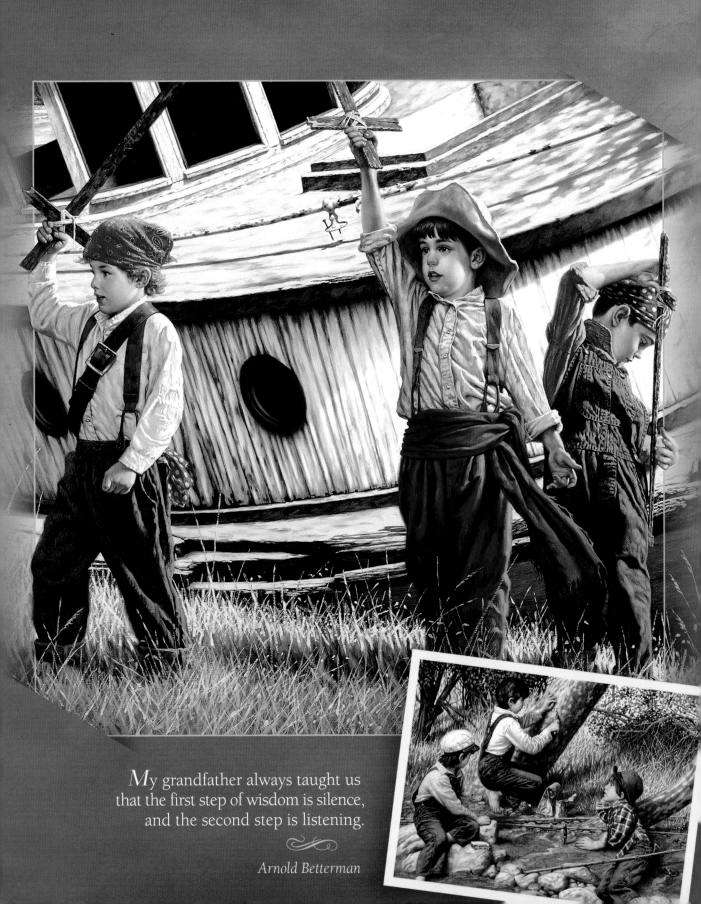

My grandfather always taught us
that the first step of wisdom is silence,
and the second step is listening.

Arnold Betterman

The Gift of Friendship

*D*id you have a "best friend" growing up? _____

_____

Were you shy or outgoing? Serious or funny? _____

_____

What quality do you think is most important in a friend? _____

_____

Share a story about a good time with friends. _____

_____

_____

_____

_____

_____

_____

_____

Tell Me About Grandma

Grandpa, do you remember when you first met Grandma? _____

_____

What did you do on your first date? _____

_____

How did you propose? _____

_____

When and where did you get married? What did you like most about your wedding? _____

_____

What have you loved most about your shared life? _____

_____

Share with me some special memories you have about your life with Grandma. _____

_____

W here we love is home—home that
our feet may leave, but not our hearts.

Oliver Wendell Holmes Sr.

*D*o not pray for gold and jade and precious
things; pray that your children and
grandchildren may all be good.

Chinese Proverb

Your Young Family

What did you do for a living when you started your family? _____

Did Grandma work? What did she do? _____

Where was your home, and what was it like? _____

What made my mom/dad laugh when they were my age? _____

How did you spend time together as a family? _____

What are your fondest memories of raising a young family? _____

Being a Grandpa

Grandpa, do you remember when I was born? _____

_____

_____

What were you doing when you heard the news? _____

_____

_____

How is being a grandparent fun for you? _____

_____

_____

What do you like to do with your grandchildren? _____

_____

_____

What do you want your grandkids to know about you? _____

_____

_____

_____

*P*erfect love sometimes does not come until the first grandchild.

Welsh Proverb

"*F*or I know the plans I have for you," says the Lord. "They are plans
for good and not for disaster, to give you a future and a hope."

The Book of Jeremiah

Hope and a Future

Grandpa, do you remember what you dreamed about accomplishing? Have you done it?

What have you enjoyed most about your work?

On your birthdays, when you blow out the candles, what wish comes to mind?

What are your wishes for me, Grandpa? For all your grandchildren?

What are three things you still want to try, see, or do in your lifetime?

Life Lessons

What have you learned that you want to pass along to me?

_____

_____

Who gave you some of the best advice ever? What was that advice?

_____

_____

_____

Which trials made you stronger? _____

_____

_____

What do you want me to know when I am choosing a career
or life path? _____

_____

_____

_____

What do you hope that I will learn early in life? _____

_____

_____

_____

*I*n early childhood you may lay the foundation of poverty or riches, industry or idleness, good or evil, by the habits to which you train your children. Teach them right habits then, and their future life is safe.

Lydia Sigourney

*L*ife has been your art.
You have set yourself to music.
Your days are your sonnets.

Oscar Wilde

Inspiration

Grandpa, did your father teach you a special craft? _____

_____

_____

Did you enjoy painting, drawing, reading, or writing as a boy?

_____

_____

Was there a color you liked most of all? _____

What kind of music or scenery inspires you? _____

_____

_____

What do you treasure most? _____

_____

_____

_____

_____

_____

_____

Traditions to Build On

Grandpa, do you remember when you and your parents celebrated family traditions? _____

_____

Did you start new traditions when your children were born? _____

_____

_____

What legacies did your parents or grandparents pass along to you?

_____

_____

Is there a tradition you hope I will share with my children someday?

_____

_____

_____

*E*ach day of our lives we make deposits
in the memory banks of our children.

Charles R. Swindoll

Over the river, and through the wood, To grandfather's house we go;
The horse knows the way, To carry the sleigh, Through the white and drifted snow.

Lydia Marie Child, from "The New-England
Boy's Song: About Thanksgiving Day"

Happy Holidays

How did you celebrate Easter, Thanksgiving, and Christmas?

_____

_____

_____

_____

Which holiday is your favorite? _____

_____

What do you like to do now during the holidays? ____

_____

_____

What was your first Thanksgiving with Grandma like? ____

_____

_____

_____

Did you ever receive or give a gift that was extra special? ____

_____

_____

_____

_____

Changing Times

Grandpa, do you remember when there weren't computers or cell phones? _____

_____

What are the best changes that have taken place during your lifetime? _____

_____

_____

What do you miss about the old days? _____

_____

_____

In what way was your childhood a lot different than mine? _____

_____

How was it similar? _____

_____

_____

_____

*F*ond Memory brings the light
Of other days around me:
The smiles, the tears
Of boyhood's years.

Thomas Moore

There is always one moment in childhood when the door opens and lets the future in.

Graham Greene

Sharing Between Generations

Do you have something special that belonged to your mother or father? _____

_____

Tell me a story about our family, Grandpa. _____

_____

_____

Where do you keep photographs or images from your lifetime? What is your favorite photograph? _____

_____

Did you ever keep a journal? What did you like to record? _____

_____

_____

Memories are special family treasures. What memories about your parents, children, and life do you want to share with me? _____

_____

_____

_____

_____

_____

A Letter from Grandpa

Grandpa, what would you want me to know most of all?

Let your grandchildren know through words and deeds, that the bond of affection which attaches the two of you to one another can never be broken.

Arthur Kornhaber

The experiences you have had are your own greatest treasure, well worth the remembering and retelling…

Ray Mungo

I share these memories with my dear grandchild,

_____

Love,

_____